AF428764

Mirror-Pain Synesthesia: My Understanding and Coping with a Rare Condition

P D Groesbeek

Published by P D Groesbeek, 2023.

While every precaution has been taken in the preparation of this book, the publisher assumes no responsibility for errors or omissions, or for damages resulting from the use of the information contained herein.

MIRROR-PAIN SYNESTHESIA: MY UNDERSTANDING AND COPING WITH A RARE CONDITION

First edition. June 26, 2023.

Copyright © 2023 P D Groesbeek.

ISBN: 979-8223354642

Written by P D Groesbeek.

Table of Contents

To everyone dealing with this condition.

Introduction

MIRROR-TOUCH SYNESTHESIA and mirror-pain synesthesia are both forms of synesthesia that involve a mirroring of sensory experiences in response to observing others. However, there are notable differences between the two, including the type of sensations experienced and their associations with empathy.

Mirror-touch synesthesia specifically relates to touch and involves feeling tactile sensations when observing someone else being touched. This can include sensations such as touch, pressure, or even pain. It is a sensory mirroring phenomenon that occurs in response to visual stimuli.

On the other hand, mirror-pain synesthesia involves the mirroring of painful sensations observed in others. Individuals with mirror-pain synesthesia not only visually perceive the pain but also internalize and mirror it within their own sensory and emotional systems, leading to a direct experience of the observed pain as if it were happening to them.

In terms of empathy, while mirror-touch synesthesia is not associated with heightened empathy, mirror-pain synesthesia, as its name suggests, involves a strong empathetic response to the pain of others. Individuals with mirror-pain synesthesia deeply empathize with the pain they witness, experiencing emotional and physical responses that go beyond mere observation. This heightened empathetic connection blurs the boundaries between self and others, as the individual's sensory and emotional systems become intertwined with those they observe.

It is worth noting that mirror-touch synesthesia and mirror-pain synesthesia can occur independently of each other. They are distinct forms of synesthesia with different sensory associations and empathetic implications. However, both conditions highlight the fascinating ways in which our brains can perceive and respond to sensory stimuli and the complexities of synesthetic experiences.

Furthermore, mirror-touch synesthesia has been found to occur in individuals with autism spectrum disorder (ASD), a condition associated with challenges in social interaction and communication. Similarly, mirror-pain synesthesia has also been observed in individuals with ASD. This suggests that there may be shared neural mechanisms or predispositions that contribute to the development of both synesthetic experiences and autism.

Overall, studying the links between mirror-touch synesthesia and mirror-pain synesthesia provides valuable insights into the diverse range of synesthetic experiences, their associations with empathy, and their potential connections to neurodevelopmental conditions such as autism. It deepens our understanding of how the brain processes sensory information and highlights the complex interplay between perception, empathy, and synesthesia.

Chapter 1

I avoid pain, especially other's pain.

AS A YOUNG BOY I NEVER really noticed how others affected me, I always just felt very strongly about others' experiences especially when I was the observer, perhaps that was the reason I was so immersed in television, I found myself completely living in another world when I watched movies, even emotionally, I would get so emotionally invested in others happiness and pain that it always left me with an after taste of emotions when the movie was over. I had to avoid horror movies, and always lean more toward comedy, even today still as I wake up in the morning, I put on a comedy and then make coffee. I would always feel like I was crazy for getting stomach aches when my girlfriend experienced her time of the month, other times my back would hurt because her back would be in pain.

I only actually realized in my late twenties that, I couldn't watch MMA videos on YouTube or Facebook because I would cringe at the pain in all my ligaments. My hands and feet would feel the sting with every blow, so I avoided these videos at all costs, as much as I would avoid any other pain.

The more I realized I avoided others' pain, the more I became aware that I was avoiding people, especially those in pain, I became aware I was avoiding even their emotional states, As soon as I was in the presence of another person in pain I would leave with their emotions and confuse it for my own, it took me another ten years to seek an answer I desperately needed. Self-medication and drug abuse were something that became a major catalyst in my unraveling, but it also became the unraveling of what was going on with me.

I always look away from the homeless person because knowing I feel their pain doesn't take away the pain, as I look away every time The Good Doctor cuts into a patient because I feel that pain even when I fully know it isn't real. Now I know a lot of my pain and emotions weren't mine, and even more so I made others' lives difficult because of the pain I was in.

Definition of Mirror-Pain Synesthesia:

The Intersection of Sensation, Empathy, and Perception

Mirror-pain synesthesia is a fascinating and rare neurological condition that blurs the boundaries between sensory perception, emotional empathy, and physical experiences. It is characterized by the involuntary mirroring of painful sensations witnessed by an individual, leading to a cascade of empathetic responses that manifest both emotionally and physically within their own body. In essence, it is as if the individual "feels" the pain they see, experiencing it as if it were happening to them directly.

The term "synesthesia" refers to a unique sensory phenomenon where stimulation of one sensory pathway leads to the involuntary and automatic experience of another sensory perception. While various forms of synesthesia have been documented, mirror-pain synesthesia specifically focuses on the integration of pain perception and empathetic responses.

Individuals with mirror-pain synesthesia possess an extraordinary ability to empathize deeply with the pain of others. When observing someone else experiencing pain, whether it be through witnessing an injury or even seeing it depicted in a visual medium, they not only perceive the pain visually but also internalize and mirror it within their own sensory and emotional framework. This mirror effect goes beyond mere empathy and elicits a direct physical and emotional response within the individual's body.

The experience of mirror-pain synesthesia can vary in intensity and duration from person to person. Some individuals may only exhibit mild mirroring sensations, while others may have more pronounced and immersive experiences. Additionally, the specific triggers for mirroring can differ, with some individuals being more susceptible to certain types of pain or particular visual cues.

It is important to note that mirror-pain synesthesia is distinct from mere empathy or empathic pain perception. While many individuals can empathize with others and experience a sense of discomfort or sympathy when witnessing pain, mirror-pain synesthesia takes this empathetic response to a heightened level. The condition blurs the boundaries between self and other, as the individual's sensory and emotional systems become intertwined with those they observe.

Although mirror-pain synesthesia is a relatively rare condition, it has gained attention in recent years as scientists and researchers strive to understand the complexities of synesthesia and empathetic responses. Studies have indicated that there may be a genetic predisposition to the condition, suggesting that certain genes or genetic variations could contribute to its development. Environmental factors, such as early experiences or trauma, may also play a role in the manifestation of mirror-pain synesthesia, further highlighting the complex interplay between nature and nurture.

Understanding and diagnosing mirror-pain synesthesia is a delicate and empathetic process. Individuals who suspect they may have the condition should seek medical evaluation from professionals familiar with synesthesia and related phenomena. Compassionate and accurate diagnosis is crucial for validating and addressing the unique challenges faced by individuals living with mirror-pain synesthesia.

In summary, mirror-pain synesthesia represents a fascinating intersection of sensory perception, empathy, and personal experience. It highlights the intricate ways in which our brains interpret and respond to the pain of others, going beyond mere observation and evoking a deep and profound mirroring of the physical and emotional aspects of pain. By recognizing and studying this condition, we deepen our understanding of the complexities of human perception and empathetic responses, opening new avenues for support, compassion, and research within the field of synesthesia.

My Personal Introduction and Experience with Mirror-Pain Synesthesia:

My Journey of Empathy and Sensory Overlap

Allow me to share with you my personal introduction and experience with the enigmatic condition known as mirror-pain synesthesia. As an individual who has wrestled with this unique neurological phenomenon, I understand firsthand the profound impact it can have on one's perception, emotions, and daily life.

For as long as I can remember, mirror-pain synesthesia has been an integral part of my existence. From the earliest recollections of my childhood, every interaction that involved the presence of pain—be it through observing someone's injuries, watching a movie or a home video, listening to a family member recounting their injury, or even a simple thought referencing pain—has triggered a cascade of sensory and empathetic responses within me. And in 2023, the flood of videos on social media has made it increasingly more difficult to deal with these responses.

The experience is difficult to put into words, but it is as if my mind forces me to share in the pain to some extent. When witnessing someone else's pain, whether it be through visual stimuli or verbal narratives, my sensory and emotional systems become entangled, leading to an almost involuntary mirroring of the pain within my own body. It is not merely a fleeting sensation but a visceral and immersive experience that can evoke genuine physical and emotional discomfort.

These mirroring sensations can manifest in a multitude of ways. Sometimes it feels as though the pain is radiating from the exact location of the injury, while at other times, it engulfs my entire body as if I am personally enduring the distressing event. This overwhelming overlap of sensations creates a profound empathetic connection to the suffering of others, blurring the boundaries between their experiences and my own.

The impact of mirror-pain synesthesia extends far beyond the immediate moment of observation or interaction. The emotional toll can be significant, as the empathetic responses often elicit feelings of sadness, distress, or even helplessness. Additionally, the physical sensations can linger, leaving me with a sense of lingering discomfort and unease long after the triggering event has concluded.

Living with mirror-pain synesthesia has been a journey of self-discovery, resilience, and learning to navigate the intricacies of this condition. It has required developing a heightened sense of self-awareness, understanding my triggers, and employing coping strategies to manage the overwhelming mirroring sensations. Through mindfulness practices, relaxation techniques, and a deepened understanding of empathy, I have been able to cultivate a greater sense of self-compassion and acceptance.

While mirror-pain synesthesia has presented unique challenges, it has also granted me a profound ability to connect with others on a deep and empathetic level. By sharing in the pain of others, I have developed an unwavering sense of compassion and a desire to support those in need. It has opened my eyes to the power of empathy and the importance of fostering understanding and acceptance within society.

The Purpose of this Book

By sharing my personal experience with mirror-pain synesthesia, I hope to shed light on the intricacies of this condition and provide solace to individuals who may be navigating similar paths. It is my sincere belief that through knowledge, empathy, and compassionate support, we can forge a community that embraces and celebrates our unique neurological experiences.

In the following sections, we will explore the intricacies of mirrored pain synesthesia in greater detail, diving into the underlying mechanisms, coping strategies, and the correlation between this condition and individuals who identify as empaths. Together, let us embark on a transformative journey of understanding, acceptance, and resilience as we unravel the complexities of mirror-pain synesthesia and its profound impact on our lives.

Chapter 2

Understanding Mirror-Pain Synesthesia: Where Sensory Perception Meets Empathetic Reflection

Overview of Synesthesia and its Different Forms

SYNESTHESIA, A REMARKABLE sensory phenomenon, encompasses a diverse range of perceptual experiences in which stimulation of one sensory pathway triggers the automatic and involuntary perception of another sensory modality. This intriguing condition demonstrates the extraordinary plasticity and interconnectedness of the human brain. While various forms of synesthesia exist, each with its own unique perceptual pairings, we will focus our attention on the captivating world of mirror-pain synesthesia.

Detailed Explanation of Mirror-Pain Synesthesia

Mirror-pain synesthesia is an exceptional variant of synesthesia that unites the realms of sensory perception, empathy, and personal experiences. Individuals with this condition have the remarkable ability to mirror painful sensations they observe, resulting in an immersive emotional and physical experience akin to actually feeling the pain themselves. It is as if the boundaries between self and another blur, and their empathetic responses manifest as real sensory and emotional phenomena.

The Neurological Basis of the Condition

The neurological basis of mirror-pain synesthesia lies within the intricate network of the brain's sensory and empathetic processing regions. Research suggests that the mirror neuron system, a network of brain cells that activate both when we perform an action and when we observe others performing the same action, may play a crucial role in this condition. The mirror neurons, primarily located in the premotor cortex and posterior parietal cortex, allow individuals to mentally simulate observed actions, leading to a sense of embodiment and shared experiences.

In the case of mirror-pain synesthesia, the mirror neuron system appears to extend beyond mere motor actions and encompasses pain perception. When individuals with this condition witness another person experiencing pain, the mirror neurons activate, triggering a cascade of neuronal firing that generates an empathetic response. This response is not limited to emotional empathy but also encompasses a somatic and sensory component, resulting in a vivid mirroring of the observed pain within the individual's own body.

The amygdala, a brain region associated with emotional processing, also plays a significant role in mirrored pain synesthesia. It helps amplify the emotional impact of the observed pain and reinforces the empathetic response, leading to a heightened emotional experience. Additionally, the insula, a region involved in both pain perception and empathy, is thought to facilitate the integration of sensory and emotional signals, further intensifying the mirroring process.

The underlying mechanisms of mirrored pain synesthesia are complex and multifaceted, involving a delicate interplay between sensory perception, emotional processing, and empathy. While research into this condition is still evolving, scientists and neurologists are making strides in unraveling its intricacies and shedding light on the fascinating neurological underpinnings that drive this unique perceptual phenomenon.

By gaining a deeper understanding of the neurological basis of mirrored pain synesthesia, we can foster empathy, compassion, and acceptance within society. Recognizing that this condition arises from the inherent interconnectedness of our brains and the profound capacity for shared experiences, we can embrace the diverse ways in which our perceptions and emotions intertwine. As we continue to delve into the complexities of mirrored pain synesthesia, we will explore coping strategies, management techniques, and the correlation with individuals who identify as empaths, ultimately striving to create a more empathetic and inclusive world for all.

Chapter 3

Signs, Symptoms, and Diagnosis

Recognizing the Signs and Symptoms of Mirror-Pain Synesthesia

RECOGNIZING THE SIGNS and symptoms of mirror-pain synesthesia is paramount to understanding and addressing this unique neurological condition. While the experiences may vary from person to person, there are common indicators that can help identify the presence of mirror-pain synesthesia.

Sensory Mirroring: The hallmark characteristic of mirror-pain synesthesia is the involuntary mirroring of painful sensations observed in others. Individuals with this condition experience a profound overlap between their own sensory perception and the pain they witness, resulting in an immersive and vivid experience of the observed pain.

Emotional Empathy: Alongside sensory mirroring, there is often a heightened emotional response among individuals with mirror-pain synesthesia. They may feel intense empathy, sadness, distress, or discomfort when witnessing or even thinking about the pain of others. The emotional connection is deeply intertwined with the sensory mirroring, amplifying the overall experience.

Physical Sensations: Mirror-pain synesthesia can manifest as physical sensations that mimic the observed pain. This can range from a localized sensation in the specific area of the observed pain to a more generalized experience throughout the body. The physical manifestations further contribute to the immersive nature of the condition.

Triggered Responses: Mirror-pain synesthesia can be triggered by various stimuli, including visual cues, verbal descriptions, or even mental imagery associated with pain. Everyday situations such as watching a movie scene depicting injury, listening to someone's account of their painful experience, or even imagining a painful scenario can evoke mirroring responses.

Common Triggers and Scenarios

Mirror-pain synesthesia can be triggered by a range of scenarios and stimuli. Understanding these common triggers provides insight into the experiences of individuals with this condition and helps facilitate a deeper understanding of their unique challenges.

Visual Stimuli: Witnessing physical injuries, seeing someone in pain, or observing pain depicted in various media forms, such as movies, videos, or images, can elicit mirror-pain sensations.

Verbal Descriptions: Listening to others recount their painful experiences, sharing stories of injuries or accidents, or engaging in conversations revolving around pain-related topics can trigger mirror-pain responses. The power of words can evoke a profound empathetic and sensory connection.

Empathetic Connections: The strength of emotional or empathetic connections plays a significant role in triggering mirror-pain synesthesia. Individuals may experience heightened mirroring sensations when witnessing pain in loved ones or feeling a close emotional bond with individuals in distress. The depth of the relationship intensifies the empathetic and sensory response.

Mental Imagery: The mere act of imagining or contemplating painful scenarios, even without any external stimuli, can evoke mirror-pain sensations in individuals with mirror-pain synesthesia. The power of the mind to recreate and simulate sensory experiences contributes to the complexity of the condition.

The Importance of Proper Diagnosis

Obtaining a proper diagnosis is crucial for individuals experiencing mirror-pain synesthesia. A diagnosis not only validates their experiences but also enables access to support, resources, and specialized care. It is essential to emphasize the significance of seeking professional help to navigate this condition effectively.

Consulting with healthcare professionals familiar with synesthesia and related conditions, such as neurologists or psychologists, can provide a comprehensive evaluation and accurate diagnosis. The diagnostic process typically involves an in-depth assessment of symptoms, medical history, and potentially additional tests or assessments, such as neuroimaging or specialized sensory tests.

A proper diagnosis offers several benefits to individuals with mirror-pain synesthesia. It helps them make sense of their experiences, fosters self-understanding, and connects them with others who share similar challenges. Diagnosis also paves the way for accessing coping strategies and management techniques tailored specifically to their needs.

By receiving a diagnosis, individuals gain validation and recognition that their experiences are real and unique. This recognition can alleviate feelings of confusion, isolation, and self-doubt, allowing them to embrace their condition with greater acceptance and self-compassion.

Furthermore, a diagnosis empowers individuals to seek appropriate support networks and communities where they can share their stories, exchange coping strategies, and learn from others' experiences. These connections can provide a sense of belonging and understanding, reducing the sense of isolation often associated with rare conditions like mirror-pain synesthesia.

Additionally, a diagnosis facilitates access to valuable resources and interventions designed to assist individuals in managing their condition effectively. Healthcare professionals can provide guidance on coping techniques, mindfulness practices, and emotional regulation strategies that can help individuals navigate the challenges of mirroring sensations.

Moreover, being diagnosed with mirror-pain synesthesia can open doors to participation in research studies aimed at deepening our understanding of the condition. By contributing to scientific advancements, individuals can actively contribute to the development of tailored treatments and interventions, potentially improving the quality of life for themselves and others affected by mirror-pain synesthesia.

In conclusion, obtaining a proper diagnosis is pivotal in the journey of individuals with mirror-pain synesthesia. It brings validation, understanding, and access to support, resources, and tailored interventions. Through a comprehensive evaluation by healthcare professionals, individuals can gain insights into their experiences, connect with a supportive community, and acquire effective coping strategies. A diagnosis empowers individuals to embrace their condition, foster resilience, and embark on a path of self-discovery and growth. With each step towards diagnosis, individuals can uncover new possibilities for managing and thriving with mirror-pain synesthesia.

Chapter 4

Causes and Triggers: *Unraveling the Complexities of Mirror-Pain Synesthesia*

Potential Genetic Factors and Predisposition

THE ORIGINS OF MIRROR-pain synesthesia are a subject of ongoing research, and while the precise causes remain elusive, there is growing evidence to suggest that genetic factors may contribute to its development. Studies have shown that individuals with a family history of synesthesia, particularly those with other forms of sensory synesthesia, may have an increased likelihood of experiencing mirrored pain synesthesia. This suggests a potential genetic predisposition that influences the wiring of the brain and the way sensory and empathetic processes interact.

Further investigations into the genetic underpinnings of mirror-pain synesthesia have revealed potential associations with specific gene variants related to synaptic transmission, neural connectivity, and sensory processing. The interplay between these genetic factors and environmental influences is likely to shape the development and manifestation of the condition.

Environmental and Developmental Influences

While genetics may lay the foundation, environmental and developmental influences also play a role in the expression of mirror-pain synesthesia. These influences can shape the intricate neural connections and contribute to the unique sensory and empathetic responses observed in individuals with the condition.

Early childhood experiences, including exposure to pain-related stimuli and the quality of social interactions, may shape the development of mirror-pain synesthesia. Research suggests that heightened sensitivity to others' pain during childhood, combined with a lack of emotional regulation skills, may contribute to the manifestation of the condition later in life. Traumatic events involving pain or witnessing distressing experiences may also influence the development and severity of mirror-pain synesthesia.

The Role of Brain Connectivity and Neural Pathways

Mirror-pain synesthesia is rooted in the complex interplay of neural pathways and connectivity within the brain. Recent neuroscientific studies have shed light on the brain regions and networks involved in the condition, offering insights into its underlying mechanisms.

The mirror neuron system, a network of brain cells primarily located in the premotor cortex and posterior parietal cortex, plays a pivotal role in mirror-pain synesthesia. This system allows individuals to mentally simulate observed actions and experiences, fostering a sense of shared embodiment. In the context of mirror-pain synesthesia, the mirror neuron system extends its reach beyond motor actions, encompassing pain perception and empathetic responses. When observing someone else experiencing pain, the mirror neurons fire, triggering a cascade of activity that leads to the mirroring of pain sensations in the individual's own body.

Additionally, brain regions such as the insula, anterior cingulate cortex, and amygdala contribute to the sensory, emotional, and affective aspects of mirror-pain synesthesia. These regions facilitate the integration of sensory information, emotional responses, and the modulation of empathetic experiences. Variations in the connectivity and activity of these brain regions may contribute to the individual differences observed in the severity and manifestations of mirror-pain synesthesia.

Understanding the intricate interplay between genetic factors, environmental influences, and brain connectivity is crucial for unraveling the causes and triggers of mirror-pain synesthesia. This multifaceted perspective allows researchers and clinicians to develop comprehensive models of the condition and explore potential avenues for intervention, coping strategies, and management techniques. By delving into the complexities of its origins, we can gain a deeper understanding of mirror-pain synesthesia and work towards improving the lives of those affected by this intriguing condition.

Chapter 5

Emotional and Physical Experiences

Emotional Responses to Mirror-Pain Sensations

MIRROR-PAIN SYNESTHESIA is not solely limited to the mirroring of physical sensations; it also encompasses a profound emotional component. The emotional responses elicited by mirrored pain sensations can be intense, complex, and deeply intertwined with the sensory experiences. Understanding these emotional responses is crucial for individuals with mirror-pain synesthesia to navigate their daily lives.

Empathy and Compassion: One of the predominant emotional responses experienced by individuals with mirror-pain synesthesia is a heightened sense of empathy and compassion. The mirroring of pain sensations often evokes a deep emotional connection to the person or situation observed, fostering a strong desire to alleviate suffering and provide support.

Distress and Discomfort: Alongside empathy, individuals with mirror-pain synesthesia may experience personal distress and discomfort. Witnessing or even imagining painful situations can trigger feelings of unease, sadness, or anxiety. The emotional intensity can vary depending on the severity and perceived impact of the observed pain.

Emotional Resilience: Over time, individuals with mirrored pain synesthesia develop strategies to manage the emotional responses associated with their condition. They may learn to navigate the delicate balance between empathetic engagement and emotional self-preservation, cultivating emotional resilience that allows them to cope more effectively with the challenges they encounter.

Physical Sensations and Their Impact on the Body

Mirror-pain synesthesia not only encompasses the mirroring of emotional experiences but also manifests in physical sensations. These physical sensations can have a profound impact on the body and significantly influence individuals' daily lives.

Sensory Overload: The mirroring of physical pain sensations can lead to sensory overload, where the body becomes overwhelmed by the intensity and volume of incoming sensory information. This overload may manifest as heightened sensitivity to touch, increased pain perception, or an amplification of other sensory experiences.

Muscle Tension and Discomfort: The physical manifestations of mirror-pain synesthesia can result in muscle tension, discomfort, or even localized pain in response to observed pain. The mirroring of physical sensations can trigger involuntary muscle contractions or a sense of heaviness in the affected body parts.

Exhaustion and Fatigue: The intense sensory and emotional experiences associated with mirror-pain synesthesia can be physically draining, leading to feelings of exhaustion and fatigue. Coping with the continuous mirroring of pain and the heightened emotional responses can consume significant energy reserves, impacting overall well-being.

Variations in Intensity and Duration

Mirror-pain synesthesia varies in terms of the intensity and duration of the experiences among individuals. Understanding these variations is essential for individuals with mirror-pain synesthesia to develop effective coping strategies and manage the condition's impact on their lives.

Intensity of Mirroring: The intensity of mirroring sensations can range from mild to severe, with some individuals experiencing a more nuanced mirroring effect and others encountering a more immersive and vivid replication of the observed pain. The degree of intensity can depend on factors such as personal sensitivity, emotional investment, and the nature of the observed pain.

Duration of Mirroring: Mirroring sensations may vary in duration, with some individuals experiencing transient mirroring that dissipates relatively quickly after exposure to the triggering stimulus, while others may have prolonged mirroring that persists for an extended period. The duration can also be influenced by individual coping strategies, environmental factors, and emotional regulation techniques.

External Factors: Various external factors can influence the intensity and duration of mirrored pain synesthesia. Stress levels, fatigue, environmental stimuli, and the overall emotional state can amplify or mitigate the mirroring effects. Individuals with mirror-pain synesthesia often develop an awareness of these external factors and learn to manage their impact on their experiences.

Chapter 6

Coping Strategies and Management Techniques: *Nurturing Resilience in Mirror-Pain Synesthesia*

Developing Self-Awareness and Acceptance

COPING WITH MIRRORED pain synesthesia begins with developing self-awareness and cultivating acceptance of one's unique experiences. By gaining a deeper understanding of the condition and acknowledging its presence, individuals can embark on a journey of self-discovery and empowerment.

Education and Information: Learning about mirror-pain synesthesia through reliable sources, support groups, and professional guidance can help individuals grasp the intricacies of their condition. By acquiring knowledge about the underlying mechanisms, common experiences, and coping strategies, individuals can better navigate their journey and develop a sense of agency.

Self-Reflection and Journaling: Engaging in self-reflection and journaling can foster self-awareness and emotional processing. By documenting thoughts, feelings, and experiences related to mirrored pain synesthesia, individuals can identify patterns, triggers, and personal coping mechanisms. This introspective practice can promote self-acceptance and a deeper understanding of their unique journey.

Seeking Support Networks: Connecting with others who share similar experiences can provide invaluable support. Joining support groups, online communities, or seeking peer-to-peer interactions can foster a sense of belonging, validation, and shared knowledge. Building a support network allows individuals to exchange coping strategies, offer encouragement, and find solace in the understanding of others who face similar challenges.

Cognitive-Behavioral Approaches to Cope with Pain Mirroring

Cognitive-behavioral approaches empower individuals with mirror-pain synesthesia to develop effective strategies for managing and mitigating the impact of pain mirroring on their daily lives. These approaches focus on changing thought patterns, beliefs, and behaviors associated with the condition.

Cognitive Restructuring: Cognitive restructuring involves identifying and challenging negative thoughts and beliefs related to pain mirroring. By replacing irrational or distressing thoughts with more balanced and realistic ones, individuals can reduce emotional distress and improve their overall well-being.

Behavioral Techniques: Engaging in behavioral techniques can help individuals regulate their responses to pain mirroring. This may include implementing relaxation exercises, engaging in distracting activities, or practicing gradual exposure to triggering stimuli. By modifying behaviors and responses, individuals can exert more control over their experiences and reduce the impact of mirroring sensations.

Emotional Regulation Strategies: Developing emotional regulation skills is crucial for individuals with mirror-pain synesthesia. Techniques such as deep breathing exercises, mindfulness practices, and grounding techniques can help individuals manage and regulate intense emotional responses. These strategies enable individuals to maintain emotional balance and minimize the disruptive impact of emotional mirroring.

Mindfulness and Relaxation Techniques

Mindfulness and relaxation techniques are powerful tools for individuals with mirror-pain synesthesia to cultivate a sense of calm, reduce stress, and enhance overall well-being.

Mindfulness Meditation: Mindfulness meditation involves focusing one's attention on the present moment without judgment. By practicing mindfulness, individuals can observe their mirroring sensations without getting entangled in them. This cultivates a sense of detachment, allowing individuals to navigate their experiences with greater equanimity and reduced distress.

Progressive Muscle Relaxation: Progressive muscle relaxation techniques involve systematically tensing and relaxing muscle groups throughout the body. This practice promotes physical relaxation, reduces muscle tension, and helps individuals manage the physical manifestations of mirror-pain synesthesia. By consciously releasing tension from the body, individuals can alleviate physical discomfort and promote a sense of ease.

Holistic Approaches: Exploring holistic approaches, such as yoga, acupuncture, massage therapy, or aromatherapy, can complement coping strategies for mirror-pain synesthesia. These practices promote relaxation, reduce stress, and enhance overall well-being. Integrating holistic approaches into one's routine can provide additional support in managing the challenges associated with the condition.

Chapter 7

Seeking Support

The Importance of a Support System

LIVING WITH MIRROR-pain synesthesia can be both challenging and isolating, but having a strong support system can make a significant difference in an individual's journey. Building and nurturing a support network can provide validation, understanding, and a sense of belonging.

Emotional Validation: A support system comprising understanding individuals who acknowledge and validate the experiences of those with mirror-pain synesthesia can be immensely beneficial. Being able to share and express emotions without judgment or skepticism helps individuals feel seen, heard, and understood.

Encouragement and Empathy: Supportive individuals can offer encouragement, empathy, and compassion, fostering a sense of hope and resilience. Their understanding and willingness to listen can provide solace during challenging times, helping individuals feel less alone in their journey.

Practical Assistance: A support system can also offer practical assistance, whether it be in accompanying individuals to medical appointments, helping with everyday tasks during times of distress, or simply providing a safe space to express oneself openly.

I know most people find it hard to understand the condition that was the exact reason I kept it to myself for so long, I didn't understand it myself at that time, how could I expect someone else to? As soon as I realised there are others that related, as well as being albe to talk about it made it easier to manage how I deal with the pain when it does hit, especially around others.

Communicating with Family, Friends, and Healthcare Professionals

Effective communication with family, friends, and healthcare professionals plays a vital role in navigating mirror-pain synesthesia. Clear and open communication helps in fostering understanding, empathy, and collaborative support.

Educating Loved Ones: Sharing information about mirror-pain synesthesia with family and friends can enhance their understanding of the condition. Providing educational resources, discussing personal experiences, and addressing any misconceptions can lay the foundation for empathy and support from loved ones.

Expressing Needs and Boundaries: Communicating personal needs and boundaries is crucial in maintaining healthy relationships. Individuals with mirrored pain synesthesia should feel empowered to express their limitations, triggers, and preferences to ensure that their support system can accommodate and respect their unique experiences.

Collaborating with Healthcare Professionals: Effective communication with healthcare professionals is essential for receiving appropriate care and support. Clearly articulating symptoms, concerns, and treatment preferences can facilitate a collaborative approach to managing mirrored pain synesthesia. Open dialogue and shared decision-making empower individuals to actively participate in their healthcare journey.

Joining Support Groups and Online Communities

Joining support groups and online communities specific to mirror-pain synesthesia can provide a sense of community, shared experiences, and valuable insights. Connecting with others who face similar challenges can be profoundly comforting and empowering.

Peer Support and Understanding: Interacting with individuals who share similar experiences fosters a sense of camaraderie and understanding. Joining support groups or online communities allows for the exchange of coping strategies, validation of experiences, and mutual encouragement.

Shared Resources and Information: Support groups and online communities often serve as valuable platforms for sharing resources, research updates, and practical tips for managing mirrored pain synesthesia. This collective knowledge enhances individuals' understanding of their condition and equips them with a wealth of information to explore.

Emotional Resilience and Empowerment: Being part of a supportive community can bolster emotional resilience and empower individuals to advocate for themselves. Engaging in discussions, sharing personal stories, and offering support to others not only builds connections but also reinforces a sense of strength and purpose.

Chapter 8

Living with Mirror-Pain Synesthesia: *Navigating Challenges and Embracing Resilience*

Daily Challenges and Adjustments

LIVING WITH MIRROR-pain synesthesia presents individuals with a unique set of daily challenges that require adjustments and adaptations. Understanding these challenges and finding effective strategies to navigate them is essential for maintaining a fulfilling life.

Sensory Overload Management: Mirror-pain synesthesia can lead to sensory overload, where external stimuli trigger intense mirroring sensations. In today's digital age, social media platforms and online content expose individuals to a plethora of visual stimuli. Managing the impact of visual stimuli is crucial for individuals with mirrored pain synesthesia. Strategies may include limiting screen time, curating social media feeds to minimize triggering content, and using content filtering tools to create a safer online environment.

Social Interactions: Interactions on social media platforms can pose additional challenges due to the potential exposure to visual stimuli that depict pain or injury. It is important for individuals to be mindful of their online engagements and to develop strategies to navigate social media responsibly. This may involve setting boundaries, using content warning filters, or seeking supportive online communities that understand and respect the challenges of mirror-pain synesthesia.

Emotional Regulation: The emotional impact of both physical and visual mirroring experiences can be overwhelming. Developing emotional regulation techniques, such as identifying triggering content and practicing self-compassion, can help individuals manage emotional responses effectively in both offline and online settings.

Exploring Personal Coping Mechanisms and Routines

Each individual with mirror-pain synesthesia develops unique coping mechanisms and routines to navigate their condition. By exploring and refining these strategies, individuals can find a sense of control and stability amidst the challenges they face.

Self-Care Practices: Engaging in self-care activities tailored to individual needs remains paramount in managing the effects of mirrored pain synesthesia, including those related to visual stimuli. This may involve incorporating practices that promote relaxation, such as meditation or spending time in nature, and adopting digital detoxes or screen-free periods to minimize the impact of visual triggers.

Adaptive Strategies: Adapting to the digital age requires individuals to employ strategies specific to managing visual stimuli. These may include adjusting screen settings to reduce brightness or filter out certain colors, using blue light-blocking glasses, or utilizing accessibility features on devices to customize visual experiences.

Routines and Structure: Establishing routines and structure in the digital realm can help individuals maintain a sense of balance and minimize exposure to triggering visual content. This can involve scheduling dedicated time for online activities, setting boundaries on social media usage, and proactively curating online spaces to align with personal preferences and well-being.

Sharing Inspirational Stories of Individuals Living with the Condition

Share your inspirational story with individuals living with mirror-pain synesthesia, it showcases your resilience, achievement, and unique journey. These stories serve as a source of inspiration, hope, and empowerment for others facing similar challenges, including the effects of visual stimuli on social media.

Overcoming Adversity: Individuals need to share their experiences of overcoming obstacles, including the impact of visual stimuli, and embracing their condition as a part of their identity. These stories highlight the strength and determination of people who have thrived despite the challenges posed by mirror-pain synesthesia in both offline and online environments.

Pursuing Passion and Creativity: Inspirational stories delve into the ways individuals have harnessed their condition to fuel their passions and creativity, while acknowledging the impact of visual stimuli. These narratives demonstrate how mirror-pain synesthesia can be channeled into artistic expression, innovative problem-solving, and unique perspectives, even in the realm of social media.

Advocacy and Support: Stories of individuals who have become advocates for mirror-pain synesthesia, raise awareness and promote understanding of the condition. They share their journeys of advocating for improved recognition, support, and responsible use of visual content online, making a positive impact on the lives of others.

Chapter 9

Treatment Options: *Navigating the Path to Relief and Progress*

Current Medical Treatments and their Limitations

WHILE THERE IS CURRENTLY no specific cure for mirror-pain synesthesia, there are medical treatments available that aim to alleviate symptoms and improve the quality of life for individuals affected by the condition. It is important to note that the effectiveness of these treatments may vary from person to person, and what works for one individual may not work for another.

Medications: Certain medications, such as anticonvulsants or antidepressants, have been prescribed off-label to manage the symptoms of mirror-pain synesthesia. These medications may help regulate neural activity and reduce the intensity of mirroring sensations. However, it is crucial to consult with a healthcare professional experienced in treating synesthesia to assess the potential benefits and risks associated with medication use.

Non-Invasive Brain Stimulation: Techniques like transcranial magnetic stimulation (TMS) and transcranial direct current stimulation (tDCS) have shown promise in managing synesthesia symptoms by modulating brain activity. These non-invasive procedures aim to disrupt or modulate neural circuits involved in synesthetic experiences. However, further research is needed to determine their efficacy and long-term effects specifically for mirror-pain synesthesia.

Psychological Interventions and Therapies

Psychological interventions play a significant role in managing mirror-pain synesthesia and its associated emotional and physical distress. These therapies aim to help individuals develop coping mechanisms, enhance emotional regulation, and improve overall well-being.

Cognitive-Behavioral Therapy (CBT): CBT is a widely utilized therapeutic approach that focuses on identifying and modifying unhelpful thought patterns and behaviors. In the context of mirror-pain synesthesia, CBT can help individuals challenge negative thoughts related to mirroring sensations, develop effective coping strategies, and gradually reduce the emotional and physical impact of the condition.

Exposure Therapy: Exposure therapy involves gradually exposing individuals to triggering stimuli in a controlled and supportive environment. This therapeutic approach helps individuals desensitize to the mirroring sensations and reduces anxiety or distress associated with specific triggers. Exposure therapy can be tailored to address the visual stimuli component of mirrored pain synesthesia, allowing individuals to gradually build resilience and adapt to the challenges posed by online or visual content.

Potential Future Advancements and Research Prospects

The field of synesthesia research is continuously evolving, and while there is still much to be explored, there are promising areas of study that may lead to advancements in understanding and managing mirrored pain synesthesia.

Neuroplasticity and Brain Training: Research suggests that the brain's capacity for change and adaptation, known as neuroplasticity, may play a crucial role in synesthesia. Exploring brain training techniques, such as neurofeedback or neurostimulation, could provide novel avenues for modulating synesthetic experiences and potentially reducing mirrored pain sensations.

Precision Medicine and Genetic Research: Advancements in genetic research and understanding individual genetic variations may shed light on the underlying causes of mirror-pain synesthesia. This knowledge could lead to personalized treatment approaches based on an individual's genetic profile, offering more targeted and effective interventions.

Collaborative Research Efforts: Collaboration between researchers, healthcare professionals, and individuals with mirror-pain synesthesia is essential for advancing our understanding of the condition and developing innovative treatment strategies. By sharing experiences, participating in research studies, and raising awareness, individuals can actively contribute to the progress in the field and shape future treatment options.

While treatment options for mirror-pain synesthesia are currently limited, ongoing research and advancements in the field offer hope for the future. It is crucial for individuals affected by the condition to stay informed, actively engage with healthcare professionals, and participate in research opportunities to contribute to the development of effective treatment approaches. By combining medical treatments, psychological interventions, and the potential for future advancements, individuals can strive towards a better quality of life and increased well-being.

Chapter 10

Empowering Others and Raising Awareness: Creating a Supportive Community

Advocacy and Spreading Awareness about Mirror-Pain Synesthesia

ADVOCACY PLAYS A CRUCIAL role in raising awareness about mirror-pain synesthesia, fostering understanding, and creating a supportive community for individuals living with the condition. By sharing personal experiences and knowledge, individuals can empower others and inspire positive change.

Sharing Personal Stories: Personal stories have the power to resonate with others and provide a glimpse into the realities of living with mirror-pain synesthesia. By sharing their experiences, individuals can create connections, reduce stigma, and help others understand the challenges and unique perspectives associated with the condition.

Engaging in Online Platforms: Social media and online platforms provide opportunities to reach a wider audience and raise awareness about mirror-pain synesthesia. Utilizing these platforms, individuals can share educational resources, engage in conversations, and connect with others who may be experiencing similar challenges. It is important to foster a supportive and inclusive digital community that promotes empathy and understanding.

Educating Healthcare Professionals and the General Public

Educating healthcare professionals and the general public is essential to ensure that individuals with mirror-pain synesthesia receive appropriate support and understanding. By increasing awareness and knowledge, we can foster an environment of empathy and compassion.

Professional Training: Collaborating with medical institutions, psychology departments, and other relevant organizations can help develop training programs for healthcare professionals. These programs should focus on recognizing the signs and symptoms of mirror-pain synesthesia, understanding its impact on individuals' lives, and implementing appropriate care and support strategies.

Public Awareness Campaigns: Launching public awareness campaigns can help dispel misconceptions and promote understanding of mirror-pain synesthesia. These campaigns can utilize various channels such as traditional media, social media platforms, and community events to reach a broad audience and increase visibility.

Supporting Research and Participating in Clinical Studies

Advancing our understanding of mirrored pain synesthesia relies on research and clinical studies. By actively supporting and participating in research endeavors, individuals can contribute to the development of effective treatments and further our knowledge of the condition.

Research Funding: Advocacy efforts can be directed towards raising funds for research initiatives focused on mirror-pain synesthesia. Donations, fundraising events, and collaborations with research institutions can provide crucial resources for conducting studies, exploring new treatment avenues, and enhancing the overall understanding of the condition.

Participating in Clinical Studies: Individuals with mirror-pain synesthesia can consider participating in clinical studies and research projects. By volunteering to be part of these studies, individuals contribute firsthand experiences, provide valuable data, and contribute to the development of evidence-based interventions.

Empowering others and raising awareness about mirror-pain synesthesia is a collective effort. By advocating for the condition, educating healthcare professionals and the general public, and actively participating in research endeavors, individuals can make a significant impact in improving the lives of those affected by mirror-pain synesthesia.

Chapter 11

Conclusion: Embracing Growth, Encouragement, and Gratitude

AS WE REACH THE FINAL chapter of this book, it is a moment to reflect on our personal journey with mirror-pain synesthesia and the growth that has accompanied it. Throughout this exploration, we have delved into the depths of our experiences, examined the various aspects of the condition, and discovered coping strategies and support mechanisms. Now, it is time to find solace in your progress and look towards the future with renewed hope and determination.

Reflection on Personal Journey and Growth

Take a moment to reflect on how far you have come. From the earliest memories of mirroring painful sensations to the challenges faced in daily life, you have shown incredible resilience and strength. Recognize the growth that has occurred within you – the understanding gained, the coping mechanisms developed, and the resilience that has been nurtured. Your journey is a testament to the human spirit's ability to adapt and thrive, even in the face of adversity.

Encouragement and Hope for Individuals with Mirror-Pain Synesthesia

To those who are embarking on their own journey with mirror-pain synesthesia, I offer you words of encouragement and hope. You are not alone. As you navigate the complexities of this condition, remember that there is a community of individuals who understand your experiences and are ready to support you. Seek solace in their stories, find inspiration in their resilience, and draw strength from the collective understanding. With time, you will discover your unique ways of managing and finding joy despite the challenges posed by mirror-pain synesthesia.

Final Thoughts and Gratitude

In concluding this book, it is important to express gratitude – gratitude for the opportunity to share your experiences, gratitude for the support received throughout this journey, and gratitude for the resilience that resides within you. Your willingness to open up, share your story, and advocate for greater understanding has the potential to impact countless lives.

Remember that the journey does not end here. Continue to seek knowledge, explore new coping strategies, and embrace the connections formed within the community. By staying engaged, both in personal growth and in the wider realm of research and advocacy, you contribute to the collective understanding and acceptance of mirror-pain synesthesia.

Embrace the uniqueness of your journey, for it has shaped you into an individual with a profound perspective and the capacity to inspire others. Let your story be a beacon of hope for those who come after you, illuminating the path toward acceptance, resilience, and a fulfilling life despite the challenges posed by mirror-pain synesthesia.

As you close this chapter and embark on the next chapter of your life, carry with you the knowledge gained, the connections formed, and the unwavering hope that resides within your heart. Embrace the opportunities for growth, find solace in the support of your community, and continue to share your story with compassion and authenticity.

Thank you for joining me on this journey. May your path be filled with strength, joy, and a sense of purpose as you navigate the intricacies of mirrored pain synesthesia and leave a lasting impact on the world around you.

Don't miss out!

Visit the website below and you can sign up to receive emails whenever P D Groesbeek publishes a new book. There's no charge and no obligation.

https://books2read.com/r/B-A-WPDZ-YBXKC

Connecting independent readers to independent writers.

mcontent.com/pod-product-compliance
ource LLC
rg PA
)2160726
)0005B/2107